God's Rx 1

BOOK ONE

THE SILVER BULLET

by
Jonnie Wright

Copyright © 2006 by Jonnie Wright
Title by Jonnie Wright
Cover design by Laura Taylor
ISBN 0-9768950-0-5

All rights reserved. No part of this book may be reproduced or transmitted in any form or by any means, electronic or mechanical, including photocopying, recording, or any information storage and retrieval system without written permission from Jonnie Wright.

Bible quotations are taken from:

AMPLIFIED BIBLE, EASTON'S ILLUSTRATED DICTIONARY, HOLMAN CHRISTIAN STANDARD BIBLE, NEW LIVING TRANSLATION, THE MESSAGE. Copyright © 1995-2003 by *Holman Christian Standard Edition—Bible Navigator by WORDsearch Corp.*

KING JAMES VERSION, NEW AMERICAN STANDARD BIBLE, NEW INTERNATIONAL VERSION. Copyright © 1998 by Zondervan Reference Software developed from *The Holy Bible, New International Version,* Copyright © 1973, 1978, 1984 by The International Bible Society.

Send questions or comments to the author at:
info@jonniewright.com
www.jonniewright.com

Printed in the United States of America

My heartfelt gratitude goes to old and new friends who offered invaluable support, clarity, and encouragement. A gratitude "Halleluiah!" goes to Shari, Barbara, Jenny, Carol, Betty, Pastor Bill, Janice, LuAnn, Margaret, Winnie, Steven, Dave, John, and Dr. Rob.

A special note of appreciation goes to my brother, David, for without his computer assistance this book would never have been published.

TABLE OF CONTENTS

INTRODUCTION 6
HOW TO USE THIS STUDY 7
CHAPTER ONE: *GOD DECLARES JESUS IS HIS SON* ... 10
   STUDY 1: *WHO IS JESUS* 11
   STUDY 2: *WHY DID JESUS COME TO EARTH* 15
   STUDY 3: *WHAT DID JESUS' WORKS REVEAL* 18
   STUDY 4: *IS JESUS SEPARATE FROM FATHER GOD* 22
   STUDY 5: *HOW CAN A MAN BE GOD* 26
CHAPTER TWO: *GOD IDENTIFIES JESUS WITH MANY NAMES* 30
   STUDY 1: *JESUS IS THE CORNERSTONE* 31
   STUDY 2: *JESUS IS THE CHURCH* 35
   STUDY 3: *JESUS IS THE MESSIAH* 38
   STUDY 4: *JESUS IS GOD'S SON* 42
   STUDY 5: *JESUS IS THE SOURCE OF OUR FAITH* 46
CHAPTER THREE: *GOD PROVIDES JESUS AS OUR SAVIOR* 49
   STUDY 1: *WHAT IS A SAVIOR* 50
   STUDY 2: *WHERE WILL I FIND MY SAVIOR* 54
   STUDY 3: *WHO IS MY SAVIOR* 58
   STUDY 4: *HOW DOES MY SAVIOR SAVE ME* 62
   STUDY 5: *WHY DO I HAVE A SAVIOR* 66
CHAPTER FOUR: *GOD AFFIRMS THAT JESUS IS THE WAY TO HIM* 70
   STUDY 1: *JESUS IS THE WAY* 71
   STUDY 2: *JESUS IS THE LIGHT* 75
   STUDY 3: *JESUS IS THE BREAD OF LIFE* 79
   STUDY 4: *JESUS IS THE VINE* 83
   STUDY 5: *JESUS IS THE RESURRECTION.* 87
APPENDIX A: *MEMORIZING SCRIPTURE* 90
APPENDIX B: *READER'S GUIDE* 95
GOD'S RX SERIES 116
ORDER INFORMATION 118

INTRODUCTION

Anyone who struggles with chronic pain has searched for the silver bullet—the magic elixir that will end the incessant suffering and return one's life to normal. If we search for God's prescription, however, we will soon discover that our silver bullet is not a medication, a therapy, an exercise regime, a seminar, a new mechanical manipulation, an operation, or even the latest, greatest cure-all potion offered by marketing enterprises. Instead, God's prescription is a relationship with a person, Jesus Christ.

Being called a "Christian" is to declare a personal relationship with Jesus Christ and to be one of His peculiar people: *"Looking for that blessed hope, and the glorious appearing of the great God and our Saviour Jesus Christ; Who gave himself for us, that he might redeem us from all iniquity, and purify unto himself a peculiar people, zealous of good works."* (Titus 2:13-14 KJV) Christians are distinctive and have hope where others would find none. *The Silver Bullet* is a devotional Bible study designed to increase spiritual hope in Jesus Christ despite one's physical condition.

So let's not be fooled by the world's promises of quick fixes and magic cures. Our endurance is in Jesus Christ, who gives us assurance of a spiritually fruitful life no matter what our circumstances may be. God does not *waste* anyone's suffering, but rather uses it for His purposes: *"As the rain and the snow come down from heaven, and do not return to it without watering the earth and making it bud and flourish... so is my word that goes out from my mouth: It will not return to me empty, but will accomplish what I desire and achieve the purpose for which I sent it."* (Isa. 55:10-11 NIV) Let's use God's antidote, Jesus Christ, as our sought after silver bullet.

HOW TO USE THIS STUDY

While physical distress can make commitment to a daily Bible study difficult, the amount of time and energy needed to do each devotional Bible study is flexible. Each Chapter has five studies broken into smaller units that can be done daily or all at one time. God treasures every moment you spend with Him. He is not bound by "shoulds" nor *should* you be. Your quest for spiritual health will occur through Holy Spirit power as you commit spending time with your habit-forming God—be it an hour or ten minutes.

Each chapter is progressive, intended to examine who Jesus Christ is, and how His power is enabling despite daily health issues. Scripture verses from different Bible translations are quoted to enrich your comprehension, application, and worship. The translations used are identified as: *Amplified Bible* (**AB**), *Holman Christian Standard Bible* (**HCSB**), *King James Version* (**KJV**), *New American Standard Bible* (**NASB**), *New International Version* (**NIV**), and *New Living Translation* (**NLT**). Although *The Message*, by Eugene H. Peterson, (NavPress, Copyright © 2002), is not a literal translation of the Bible, selected passages are included for their lyrical quality and graphic word pictures (**Msg**).

The commentary and questions resulting from the quoted Scripture verses are designed to increase your understanding and to apply scriptural truth to your circumstances and relationships. The following sections are found in each study. They may be done separately or be combined in any order. Each section provides further opportunities for applying Godly principles to your day-to-day living.

SCRIPTURE PASSAGE is the context from which the devotional study verse is taken. After reading the suggested verses, there are several questions, based on the NIV translation, to further assist you in your comprehension and application of the text.

MEMORIZING SCRIPTURE is nourishment for your emotional, mental, spiritual, and physical well-being. Techniques for memorizing Scripture can be found in **Appendix A,** pages 90-94.

TODAY'S CHALLENGE reminds you to reflect on the biggest potential trial of the day. How do you plan to manage this thorny circumstance? What attitude do you need to adjust so that this difficulty will be a Jesus-event rather than a crisis?

PRAYER PARTNER'S NEEDS is an opportunity to commit to praying for another person's spiritual and physical needs, as well as your own. Reciprocal sharing of concerns with someone once a week and a commitment to pray for this person will help you stay accountable for the daily goals God prompts you to set.

IN JESUS' NAME offers suggestions for acts of kindness on those days when symptoms and pain recede. God has already prepared you for each good work you accomplish. Many more ideas may be found in *Beyond Casseroles: 505 ways to encourage a Chronically Ill Friend*, by Lisa J. Copen, (Rest Ministries, Copyright © 2005).

READER'S GUIDE is **Appendix B**, pages 95-115, and offers supplementary information for both small group leaders and the individual learner. Questions addressed in the Reader's Guide will have 📖 before the question number.

No matter how many *how-to* books we have "under our belts," the bottom line is living out the concepts, insights, and reflections we discover when searching for Godly answers. Scripture points us to the solution for our daily struggles. The answer is Jesus Christ.

CHAPTER ONE

God declares Jesus is His Son.

To know Jesus Christ is to know God. This knowledge enables us to experience and savor our life even with a chronic condition. How is that feasible? It is possible when we apply Christ's words of truth and promises to our everyday living. God's words can spiritually move us beyond the limitations of our physical suffering.

We begin our study in Exodus with God identifying Himself to Moses: *"I-AM-WHO-I-AM... The LORD, the God of your fathers—the God of Abraham, the God of Isaac and the God of Jacob... This is my name forever, the name by which I am to be remembered from generation to generation."* (Ex. 3:14-15 NIV) This same God, centuries later, tells us who Jesus is when He is baptized, *"You are my Son, whom I love; with you I am well pleased."* (Mark 1:11 NIV), and when His human appearance is altered on the Mount of Transfiguration, *"This is my Son, whom I love. Listen to him!"* (Mark 9:7 NIV)

In this chapter, we'll study Jesus Christ's relationship to God so that we may practice applying scriptural truth to our daily needs.

There is one prayer that God must answer, and that is the prayer of Jesus.

Oswald Chambers, *So I Send You*, 1930.

STUDY 1: *Who is Jesus?*

"Jesus said unto them, 'Verily, verily, I say unto you, Before Abraham was, I am.'" (John 8:58 KJV)

When Jesus pronounced that He had the same name as God, the Jewish leaders of the day wanted to stone Him for blasphemy. Jesus called Himself, "I am," which is the same name God used when speaking to Moses. If Jesus declared Himself to have the same name as God, then He was declaring that He was God. Angering the Jews further was the fact that Jesus put Himself before Abraham chronologically, making Himself more important than the Patriarch of Judaism. The synagogue leaders—who were the scribes, the Pharisees, and the Sadducees—could not grasp how Jesus, appearing as a man, could possibly be their expected Savior, the Messiah. (See Appendix B, page 98 for more background information.)

1. Jesus declares that He and Father God are the same by using God's name, I-AM. What does that scriptural claim mean to you?

2. What does *blasphemy* mean? (See Appendix B, page 99.)

3. Do you depend on a certain Biblical promise when you're having a difficult day? Which one and why? If not, what do you depend on? (See Appendix B, page 99.)

Scripture Passage: John 8:48-59 NIV

4. How did the Jewish leaders respond to Jesus' claim of being God? (v. 59)

5. The Jewish leaders' made three statements revealing their unbelief? State them in your own words. (v. 48, 53, 57)

   ➤

   ➤

   ➤

6. What three statements did Jesus make about God and/or Himself? State these in your own words. (v. 51, 54, 58)

   ➤

   ➤

   ➤

7. Jesus drew a virtual line in the sand stating that He is God. If you believe His statement as truth, then you have eternal life. (See Appendix B, page 99.)

a. What happens if you disbelieve?

b. Can you believe a little bit? How?

Memory Verse: *"No one has ever seen God, but God the One and Only, who is at the Father's side, has made him known."* (John 1:18 NIV)
(See Appendix A, pages 90-94 for memorizing tips.)

Today's Challenge: (See page 8.)

1. How will you cope?

2. What will be your attitude?

Prayer Partner's needs: (See page 8.)

➤

➤

In Jesus' Name: (activities for a good day) (See page 9.)

1. Scour flea markets, garage sales, or thrift shops looking for a cute pot to decorate. Spruce up the outside by gluing on ribbons, nuts, bolts, flowers, nails, or toothpicks. For the inside, fill with real or artificial flowers, weeds, mismatched tools, figurines, marbles, or pipe-cleaner figures and give it to a shut-in or sick friend who needs a good laugh.

2. Reflect on Martin Luther King Jr.'s statement concerning the story of the Good Samaritan: "The first question that the priest and the Levite asked was: 'If I stop to help this man, what will happen to me?' But... the good Samaritan reversed the queston: 'If I do not stop to help this man, what will happen to him?'"

3. Remember what you loved to do as a child. Reclaim some of that delight by starting a collection—dolls, stamps, bullets—or take up a hobby—making miniatures of airplanes, cars, or dollhouses, doing puzzles, dancing, painting, singing.

STUDY 2: *Why did Jesus come to earth?*

"No man has ever seen God at any time; the only unique Son, or the only begotten God, Who is in the bosom [in the intimate Presence] of the Father, He has declared Him [He has revealed Him and brought Him out where He can be seen; He has interpreted Him and He has made Him known]." (John 1:18 AB)

God created mankind for divine fellowship. In Genesis, God had Adam name all the livestock, beasts of the field, and birds of the air. (Gen. 2:20) God was Creator, yet He allowed His creation Adam to name all that He had made. This action by God emphasizes the level of friendship He desires with us. When Adam chose to disobey God—by eating fruit from the forbidden tree—Adam's sin lost our intimate access to God. How can we sinners now approach our Holy God? We cannot unless we too are holy. Jesus Christ renewed the intimacy for us by His life, His death, and His resurrection. He *declared, revealed, brought out,* and *interpreted* who God is so that we can, once again, have intimacy with Him.

1. Jesus Christ reveals to us who God is. Rewrite today's Scripture replacing the pronouns *He* and *Him* with the words *the Father* or *Christ.* Remember that Jesus is *"the only unique Son, or* the only begotten God."
   (See Appendix B, page 100 for the answer.)

   Here's how it starts:

   "No man has ever seen God at any time; *the only unique Son, or* the only begotten God, Who is in the bosom [in the intimate Presence] of the Father, **Christ** has declared **the Father** [**Christ** has revealed

2. Are you preoccupied with such things as over-eating, shopping, working, smoking, watching TV, reading the newspaper, exercising, playing computer games, etc. When can these activities interfere with experiencing God more intimately?

3. How did God make His presence known when you had a medical emergency?

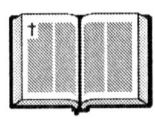

Scripture Passage: John 1:1-18 NIV

4. What did John the Baptist say about Jesus? (v. 15)

5. What was given through Moses? (v. 17)
(See Appendix B, page 101.)

   a. What came through Jesus Christ? (v. 17)

   b. What is the difference between the Law of Moses and the Grace of Jesus?

Memory Verse: *"No one has ever seen God, but God the One and Only, who is at the Father's side, has made him known."* (John 1:18 NIV)
(See Appendix A, pages 90-94 for memorizing tips.)

Today's Challenge: (See page 8.)

1. How will you cope?

2. What will be your attitude?

Prayer Partner's needs: (See page 8.)

➤

➤

In Jesus' Name: (See pages 9.)

1. Sort photo or digital pictures with a friend and share your good times.
2. Write down responses to thoughtless and hurtful remarks people make.

STUDY 3: *What did Jesus' works reveal?*

Jesus said, "…*do you say of Him, whom the Father sanctified and sent into the world, 'You are blaspheming,' because I said, 'I am the Son of God'? If I do not do the works of My Father, do not believe Me; but if I do them, though you do not believe Me, believe the works, that you may know and understand that the Father is in Me, and I in the Father.*" (John 10:36-38 NASB)

Jesus began His ministry at the age of thirty, the age acceptable for a Jewish man to become a Rabbi or teacher. The authenticity of His authority could not be denied nor His very public miracles ignored. The Jewish leaders were alarmed by Jesus' growing popularity with the masses and feared losing their influence with the Jewish community and with the governing Romans. They were, however, no match for Jesus since He was indeed divine and His miracles and works were His credentials to the believing and unbelieving alike.

1. Name three miracles Jesus performed:
   (See Appendix B, page 101.)

   ➢

   ➢

   ➢

   a. Who made these miracles possible?

   b. If these events happened today would you recognize God's hand? Explain.

2. Jesus did the work God planned for Him.
(See Appendix B, page 101.)

   a. What was that work?

   b. Are you doing the work God planned for you? What is that work?

   c. Does your pain help or hinder your God-inspired work?

Scripture Passage: John 10:22-39 NIV

3. The Jewish leaders were frustrated when their plans to discredit Jesus were thwarted. When does frustration overwhelm you?

4. Does anything about your physical condition make you feel helpless? What?

5. What are three practical actions you can take when you are feeling frustrated or helpless?

   ➢

   ➢

   ➢

6. Who are Jesus' sheep? (v. 25-26)

   a. What do Jesus' sheep do? (v. 27)

   b. What does Jesus give His sheep? (v. 28)

   c. What won't happen to God's sheep? Why? (v. 28-30)

Memory Verse: "*No one has ever seen God, but God the One and Only, who is at the Father's side, has made him known.*" (John 1:18 NIV)

(See Appendix A, pages 90-94 for memorizing tips.)

Today's Challenge: (See page 8.)

1. How will you cope?

2. What will be your attitude?

Prayer Partner's needs: (See page 8.)

➤

➤

In Jesus' Name: (activities for a good day) (See page 9.)

1. Write a thank you card or send an email to someone who has brought you joy in the last week. Use words such as: *delight, elation, enjoyment, gladness, happiness, joyfulness, pleasure,* and *encouragement.*

2. Buy a bright colored umbrella to remind you of a rainbow and God's promises.

STUDY 4: *Is Jesus separate from Father God?*

Jesus said, *"Do you not believe that I am in the Father, and that the Father is in Me? What I am telling you I do not say on My own authority and of My own accord; but the Father Who lives continually in Me does the (His) works (His own miracles, deeds of power)."* (John 14:10 AB)

A mental picture of Jesus' qualities can be perfectly superimposed over those of our Holy God—they cannot be separated. Yet Jesus walked and talked as a man. Isaiah explains why we don't understand this seeming paradox of God as Father and God as Son: *"'For my thoughts are not your thoughts, neither are your ways my ways,' declares the LORD. 'As the heavens are higher than the earth, so are my ways higher than your ways and my thoughts than your thoughts.'"* (Isa. 55:8-9 NIV) Jesus' life, death and resurrection reveal an exact representation of God's character and authority. Only God would be able to describe and model Himself accurately for mankind.

1. Read Matt. 8:1-3, Matt. 10:1, Matt. 14:25-31, and John 11:39-44. What were some of the *miracles and deeds of power* that Jesus did that *only* God could do?
(See Appendix B, page 102.)

2. Name at least one *good* experience you've had while being unwell that could not have happened had you been healthy.

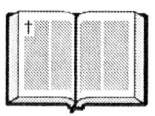

Scripture Passage: John 14:8-21 NIV

3. Who must you have faith in? (v. 12)

   a. How can you bless others with that faith? (v. 12-14)

   b. How would your healing bring glory to God?

   c. How does your current chronic condition glorify God?

4. Jesus promised His disciples that God the Father would send another to comfort them. (v. 16-17) Who is this Comforter?

   a. Where will this Comforter live? How long?

   b. How will the world react?

5. Jesus said, "...*the Father will give you whatever you ask in my name.*" (John 15:16b NIV) Does this mean that God will not give you what you do not ask for? Explain your answer. (See Appendix B, page 102.)

6. How intimate must you be with Jesus Christ before you can use His name in a conversation with God? (See Appendix B, page 102.)

   a. Why do you think so?

   b. What steps can you take to increase your fellowship with Jesus?

Memory Verse: "*No one has ever seen God, but God the One and Only, who is at the Father's side, has made him known.*" (John 1:18 NIV)
(See Appendix A, pages 90-94 for memorizing tips.)

Today's Challenge: (See page 8)

1. How will you cope?

2. What will be your attitude?

Prayer Partner's needs: (See page 8)

➤

➤

In Jesus' Name: (activities for a good day) (See page 9)

1. Trust spontaneity: find a friend or coworker who is available, search fridge and cupboards for picnic fare, and go off to the park or other restful place for an unplanned lunch.

2. Write an article for the church bulletin or newsletter sharing a topic for which you have a passion.

STUDY 5: *How can a man be God?*

"They all asked, 'Are you then the Son of God?' He replied, 'You are right in saying I am.'" (Luke 22:70 NIV)

There are two statements of truth found in Jesus' short answer to the question the religious leaders asked Him on the morning of His crucifixion. The first is Jesus' confirmation that indeed He was—and is—the Son of God. And then He said, "I am," using God's name as His own. Jesus knew what kind of response He would receive when claiming to be the Son of God. He already knew the religious leaders would take Him to Governor Pilate and He would be crucified. His last hours on earth were excruciatingly painful as spikes in His hands and feet secured Him to a standing cross. Jesus experienced physical agony as He was left on the cross to die. He knows pain.

1. If you had to answer the question, "Are you a Christian?" knowing that you would be executed, explain how you would answer.

2. It doesn't seem fair that Jesus, who had no sin, should suffer with pain then die for all sin. Does your pain and suffering seem fair or unfair? Why do you think so?

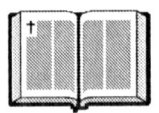

Scripture Passage: Luke 22:66-23:1 & Luke 23:32-43 NIV

3. Two criminals were crucified with Jesus that day, each taking a different viewpoint concerning Jesus' punishment. (Luke 23:39-42)

   a. Describe a time in your life when your attitude resembled the first criminal.

   b. What has happened in your life to inspire you to agree with the second criminal?

4. Many prophecies of the coming of a Messiah who could free the Jewish people from bondage may be found in the Old Testament. Read Isa. 53:10-12, then answer the following questions:

   a. Who decided how Christ would die? (v. 10)

   b. What would Jesus do for the many? (v. 11)

   c. How did God reward Jesus' suffering? (v. 12)

   d. What did Christ do for the transgressors? (v. 12)

e. How do you treat someone who has upset you?

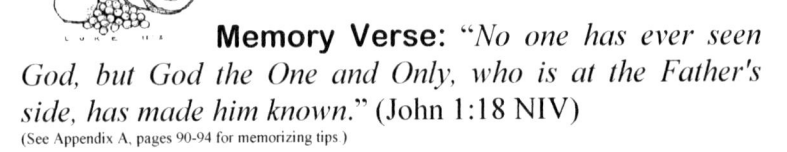

Memory Verse: *"No one has ever seen God, but God the One and Only, who is at the Father's side, has made him known."* (John 1:18 NIV)
(See Appendix A, pages 90-94 for memorizing tips.)

Today's Challenge: (See page 8.)

1. How will you cope?

2. What will be your attitude?

Prayer Partner's needs: (See page 8.)

➢

➢

In Jesus' Name: (activities for a good day) (See page 9.)

1. Send tapes of missed church services to an elderly shut-in or a convalescing person.

2. Learn a new craft or a new skill.

3. Present a friend who is over-burdened with job and family commitments a box of greeting cards and wrapping paper for every occasion so that he or she will have them on hand for forgotten, last-minute events.

4. Rewrite the following Scripture God spoke to Isaiah, making each verse a personal activity you could do. For example, the phrase *"loose the chains of injustice"* might be rewritten as: I will write a letter to my representative in Congress on an issue that concerns me. (Leader, see Appendix B, page 102 for suggestions on group application.)

> *"Is not this the kind of fasting I have chosen:*
> *to loose the chains of injustice*
> *and untie the cords of the yoke,*
> *to set the oppressed free*
> *and break every yoke?*
> *Is it not to share your food with the hungry*
> *and to provide the poor wanderer with shelter--*
> *when you see the naked, to clothe him,*
> *and not to turn away from your own flesh and blood?*
> *Then your light will break forth like the dawn,*
> *and your healing will quickly appear;*
> *then your righteousness will go before you,*
> *and the glory of the LORD will be your rear guard."*
> (Isa. 58:6-8 NIV)

CHAPTER TWO

God identifies Jesus with many names.

Throughout both Old and New Testaments, Jesus has been identified with more than one hundred different names: precious cornerstone, Messiah, the Christ, Son of the living God, Immanuel, King of the Jews, author and perfector of our faith, the head of the church, and many more. Names are meaningful to God, as evidenced in John's Gospel: *"But these are written that you may believe that Jesus is the Christ, the Son of God, and that by believing you may have life in his name."* (John 20:31 NIV)

God exalts Jesus by giving His Name power over all other names: *"Therefore God exalted him to the highest place and gave him the name that is above every name, that at the name of Jesus every knee should bow, in heaven and on earth and under the earth, and every tongue confess that Jesus Christ is Lord, to the glory of God the Father."* (Phil. 2:9-11 NIV) Jesus' many names reveal the character and attributes of our God. When pain threatens to take over our horizon, knowing His qualities will remind us that He is bigger than our circumstances.

The joy of anything, from a blade of grass upwards, is to fulfill its created purpose.

Oswald Chambers, *The Love of God*, 1938.

STUDY 1: *Jesus is the Cornerstone.*

"Therefore the Lord GOD said: 'Look, I have laid a stone in Zion, a tested stone, a precious cornerstone, a sure foundation; the one who believes will be unshakable. And I will make justice the measuring line and righteousness the mason's level…" (Isa. 28:16-17a HCBS)

In the prophet Isaiah's day, temples were built of stone. Yet in this passage, Isaiah foretells the building of a new temple—not constructed out of stone but hearts. God is the architect and has established His church through Jesus Christ, so that it is *tested, precious, sure, unshakable,* and made of *justice* and *righteousness.* God will measure all believers using Jesus as the standard so that the building of His kingdom will last for eternity. (See Appendix B, page 103 for further commentary.)

1. Jesus is the perfect cornerstone with which to build God's spiritual church.

   a. What is one thing God is doing right now to shape and strengthen you in your faith so that you will fit into His non-denominational, Kingdom-of-God church?

   b. Which activity would ease some of the emotional stresses you are feeling: exercising at the gym, shopping for a red hat, taking a walk with a loved one, writing a short note to a friend, calling an encouraging relative, emailing a note to a caring co-worker, or…?

2. Peter states: *"As you come to him, the living Stone—rejected by men but chosen by God and precious to him—you also, like living stones, are being built into a spiritual house..."* (1 Peter 2:4-5a NIV) Sketch a church made of stones or bricks—label Jesus' stone and your own.

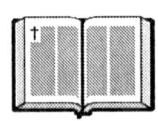

Scripture Passage: Matt. 5:1-16 NIV

3. Identify and explain three examples of how the words of Jesus have helped you live—for example: I've been *meek* and not arrogant with my boss, I've been God's *light* to my unsaved relative, or I will not *worry* about my finances since God will teach me how to budget.

   ➢

   ➢

   ➢

4. Read Job 38:1-11 then answer the following questions.

   a. What can God do that man cannot? (v. 4, 8)

b. In considering your chronic condition, what can God do that you cannot?

c. What event is prophesized in verses 6 and 7?

Memory Verse: *"The LORD is my light and my salvation—whom shall I fear? The LORD is the stronghold of my life—of whom shall I be afraid?"* (Ps. 27:1 NIV)
(See Appendix A, pages 90-94.)

Today's Challenge:

1. How will you cope?

2. What will be your attitude?

Prayer Partner's needs:

➤

➤

In Jesus' Name: (activities for a good day)

1. Visit a friend who's going through a tough time. Bring a tea set and make it tea time, or bring a coffee machine and make lattes.

2. Plant flower bulbs in the fall. Watch God's miracle of life as winter and its barren soil give way to His creation in spring.

3. Offer to house-sit. New surroundings may help perk you up.

4. Contemplate the gifts of love and kindness done by friends. Choose your favorite act of love and pass it on.

5. Check grocery ads for "buy one, get one free" coupons. Give the extra one to a needy friend, a local church who has a food bank, or donate it to a homeless shelter.

6. When reading your favorite magazine, look for articles that will encourage others, cut them out, and mail with a note of encouragement.

7. Organize a *love-month* for someone who is struggling with difficult circumstances. Coordinate friends and relatives to send a note, visit, or call each day for a month.

8. Visit your local library and peruse their DVD and books-on-tape collection. Make a list of what you would like to see, hear, or read. Use the library for free entertainment.

STUDY 2: *Jesus is the Church.*

"And God placed all things under his feet and appointed him to be head over everything for the church, which is his body, the fullness of him who fills everything in every way." (Eph. 1:22-23 NIV)

Is the church a building? Not in God's eyes. He has, is, and will continue to construct a spiritual church established on the cornerstone of Jesus Christ. The church is not a building but a living organism with Jesus as the head and believers as the body. Our spiritual worth to holy God is far greater then how many church events we attend or ministries we do because He is God of the spirit not God of the flesh.

1. Name one church event in which you have seen God at work.

2. In which church activities is it difficult for you to participate? (See Appendix B, page 103.)

    a. How do you compensate or overcome your restricted participation?

    b. How does that make you feel?

Scripture Passage: Eph. 1:11-23 NIV

3. Why were you included in Christ? (v. 13)

    a. How were you marked?

    b. Who is the seal?

4. In Paul's prayer, he asks God for many spiritual gifts for you.

    a. What are some of them? (v. 17-19)

    b. In dealing with health issues, which gifts would you desire?

    c. How might God's answer to the desire of your heart look different from what you expect or want?

5. What did Christ receive from God? (v. 22-23)

Memory Verse: *"The LORD is my light and my salvation—whom shall I fear? The LORD is the stronghold of my life—of whom shall I be afraid?"* (Ps. 27:1 NIV)

(See Appendix A, pages 90-94.)

Today's Challenge:

1. How will you cope?

2. What will be your attitude?

Prayer Partner's needs:

➤

➤

In Jesus' Name: (See pages 29 or 69.)

37
Chapter Two

STUDY 3: *Jesus is the Messiah.*

"The first thing Andrew did was to find his brother Simon and tell him, 'We have found the Messiah (that is, the Christ).'" (John 1:41 NIV)

Easton's Illustrated Dictionary chronicles the Biblical prophesies of the Messiah. "The first great promise (Gen 3:15) contains in it the germ of all the prophecies recorded in the Old Testament regarding the coming of the Messiah and the great work he was to accomplish on earth. The prophecies became more definite and fuller as the ages rolled on; the light shone more and more unto the perfect day. Different periods of prophetic revelation have been pointed out, (1) the patriarchal; (2) the Mosaic; (3) the period of David; (4) the period of prophetism, i.e., of those prophets whose works form a part of the Old Testament canon. The expectations of the Jews were thus kept alive from generation to generation, till the "fulness of the times," when Messiah came, "made of a woman, made under the law, to redeem them that were under the law." In him all these ancient prophecies have their fulfilment. Jesus of Nazareth is the Messiah, the great Deliverer who was to come. (Compare Mat 26:54; Mark 9:12; Luke 18:31; Luke 22:37; John 5:39; Acts 2; Acts 16:31; Acts 26:22, 23)"

How did the Jewish leaders of the day miss what is so obvious to us—Jesus Christ is the Messiah. They wanted to be saved from the wrong thing. They wanted a warrior king to free them from Roman rule and to establish a Jewish nation. Are we any different today? Aren't we looking for freedom from pain, illness, and suffering? Let's adjust our focus from what Jesus can do *for* us and refocus on what He can do *in* us—even in the midst of our suffering.

1. What was the good news Andrew wanted to share?
(See Appendix B, page 104.)

2. Andrew shared the truth of who Jesus Christ was to his brother Peter. What was the result of this one-person evangelizing?

   a. How can you share the Gospel of Christ even when you feel unwell?

   b. Who do you know that needs this timeless message of hope?

   c. What might you say to share the truth of Jesus Christ with this person?

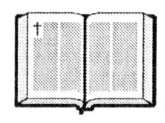

Scripture Passage: John 1:29-42 NIV

3. Who proclaimed Jesus as the Son of God before Andrew, and how did he know? (v. 32-33)

4. What did John the Baptist use to baptize repentant sinners? (v. 31) (See Appendix B, page 104.)

   a. With what does Jesus baptize? (v. 33)

   b. With what have you been baptized?

   c. How do you know?

Memory Verse: *"The LORD is my light and my salvation—whom shall I fear? The LORD is the stronghold of my life—of whom shall I be afraid?"* (Ps. 27:1 NIV)
(See Appendix A, pages 90-94.)

Today's Challenge:

1. How will you cope?

2. What will be your attitude?

Prayer Partner's needs:

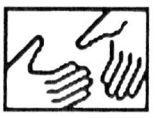

➤

➤

In Jesus' Name: (activities for a good day)

1. Help your pastor and church staff become aware of the needs of people with chronic pain. Support can be as simple as a reassuring greeting or a friendly good-bye. Other assistance could include: arranging appropriate seating for the church service, providing a prayer partner, sending a personal invitation to a Bible study group, making an in-home visit, or organizing a compassionate support group of other people who experience a chronic condition.

2. Freeze serving sizes of your favorite meal then invite an introverted friend to dinner at his/her house.

3. Assume the responsibilities for a caretaker of an adult parent, a chronically ill child, or an invalid spouse for half-an-hour or half-a-day. You will provide a blessing to someone who is in need of some well-earned free time.

STUDY 4: *Jesus is God's Son.*

"He [Jesus] said to them, 'But who do you say that I am?' And Simon Peter answered and said, 'Thou art the Christ, the Son of the living God.' And Jesus answered and said to him, 'Blessed are you, Simon Barjona, because flesh and blood did not reveal this to you, but My Father who is in heaven.'" (Matt. 16:15-17 NASB)

When Jesus walked on earth as the Messiah, the Christ, the Son of God, there were many rumors about who others thought He might be. Opinions differed—some said John the Baptist, others Elijah, and still others called Him a prophet. But Jesus asked His disciples, and us, a very important question: who do *we* think He is? If we agree with Peter that Jesus is *"the Christ, the Son of the living God,"* we may be sure of the forgiveness of our sins, and the knowledge of spending eternity with our God. If we do not agree, our lives will flounder with no direction and our souls will dwell in darkness forever.

1. Do you agree or disagree with Simon Peter's answer to Jesus' question? Explain your response.

2. Since you know God is listening, what would you like to ask or tell Him right now?

Scripture Passage: Matt. 16:13-20, Mark 8:27-29, Luke 9:18-24 NIV

3. You just read three accounts of the same event.
(See Appendix B, pages 104-105.)

   a. Which version has the longest account?

   b. Which version has the shortest account?

   c. What did you learn from Matthew's account that you did not from Mark's?

   d. Explain why these three Gospel books recount the same event differently.

4. The Message records Luke 9:23-24 this way: *"Anyone who intends to come with me has to let me lead. You're not in the driver's seat—I am. Don't run from suffering; embrace it. Follow me and I'll show you how. Self-help is no help at all. Self-sacrifice is the way, my way, to finding yourself, your true self."*

   a. What would it be like to have Jesus lead you in every aspect of your physical condition?

b. Does this paraphrase of Jesus' declaration make the concept of "carrying one's cross" easier to understand or more vivid? Explain.

c. What does the paraphrase of Jesus' statement, *"Don't run from suffering; embrace it. Follow me and I'll show you how"* mean to you?

d. How can you embrace suffering in your current health situation?

Memory Verse: *"The LORD is my light and my salvation—whom shall I fear? The LORD is the stronghold of my life—of whom shall I be afraid?"* (Ps. 27:1 NIV)
(See Appendix A, pages 90-94.)

Today's Challenge:

1. How will you cope?

2. What will be your attitude?

Prayer Partner's needs:

➢

➢

In Jesus' Name: (activities for a good day)

1. Offer to host a Bible study in your home.

2. Purchase a phone card and send it with a note of support to a shut-in, a relative, or a faraway friend.

3. Help your church office organize lists of available people to meet such needs as: handyman jobs, auto repair, yard work, baby-sitting, pet-sitting, and house cleaning.

4. Visit a friend who needs a pick-me-up. Bring something of yours that makes you smile and loan it to him or her for a while.

5. Plant a rosebush with a friend. Reach out to each other by sharing the "thorns" and "flowers" of your relationship.

6. Find out how to order your groceries on-line for those really tough days when shopping is out of the question.

STUDY 5: *Jesus is the Source of our faith.*

"Keeping our eyes on Jesus, the source and perfecter of our faith, who for the joy that lay before Him endured a cross and despised the shame, and has sat down at the right hand of God's throne." (Heb.12:2 HCSB)

Jesus set aside His place in heaven to be human for thirty-three years so that all of us who choose to believe may enter into the joy of being in God's throne room. As *"source and perfecter of our faith,"* Jesus wants us to believe in Him and will give us the faith to do so. He went to the cross so that we could be holy enough to be in the presence of our Holy God. How important we must be to have been chosen as God's children to live with Him for eternity. (See Appendix B, pages 105-106 for more information on crucifixion.)

1. From whom does your faith come?

2. What kind of shame must there have been to be nailed to a Roman cross?

Scripture Passage: Heb. 12:1-13 NIV

3. The author of Hebrews describes your Christian life as running a race. (v. 1-2)

    a. If your race includes hurdles, which hurdle appears to be the most difficult to get over right now?

b. Why do you think so?

4. Who does God discipline? (v. 5-6)

5. How are you to receive discipline? (v.7)

6. What is the difference between man's emotional discipline and God's loving discipline? (v. 9-10)

7. Verse eleven tells you what discipline produces. Read 1 Peter 1:6-7. Summarize God's purpose for discipline.

8. Explore your feelings concerning one of your favorite names for Jesus.

Memory Verse: *"The LORD is my light and my salvation—whom shall I fear? The LORD is the stronghold of my life—of whom shall I be afraid?"* (Ps. 27:1 NIV)
(See Appendix A, pages 90-94.)

Today's Challenge:

1. How will you cope?

2. What will be your attitude?

Prayer Partner's needs:

➢

➢

In Jesus' Name: (See pages 29 or 69.)

1. *"My comfort in my suffering is this: Your promise preserves my life."* (Ps. 119:50) Use the psalmist's words to sketch a picture, paint a bookmark, write a song, take a picture, or create a needlepoint design.

2. Clean out a drawer or closet that you've been avoiding.

CHAPTER THREE

God provides Jesus as our Savior.

It is not enough to know *about* Jesus—information is not knowledge. For Him to be our silver bullet against pain and illness, we must believe and accept as truth that Jesus carried our pain, our suffering, and our sins to the cross, that He arose alive from the burial tomb, and that He ascended into heaven and sits at the right hand of Holy God. He now dwells as God in our hearts when we invite Him to do so. We do not have to explain how these things can be, only believe that they are.

Continually restate to yourself what the purpose of your life is. The destined end of man is not happiness, nor health, but holiness... the one thing that matters is whether a man will accept the God who will make him holy. At all costs a man must be rightly related to God.

Oswald Chambers, *My Utmost for His Highest*, 1935.

STUDY 1: *What is a Savior?*

"God made him who had no sin to be sin for us, so that in him we might become the righteousness of God."
(2 Cor. 5:21 NLT)

In order to have salvation, we must have a savior—someone who can take away the darkness of our sins and present us pure before God. God's purity and holiness is like light that has no edges, no shadows, no dimness. None of us can claim to have God's purity, except Jesus Christ—who was both Son of God (Mark 1:1), and Son of Man (Luke 18:31-33). His crucifixion, death, and resurrection saved us from the eternal consequences of sin so that we could stand righteous before our pure and holy God. Jesus saved us from ourselves (Matt. 26:41), from the world (John 3:17), and from the darkness of evil (Eph. 6:12).

1. Have you confessed Jesus as your Savior?
   (See Appendix B, page 107.)

   a. Where?

   b. When?

   c. Why?

2. Besides church, where or when have you found yourself in God's presence?

3. What does the term *right with God* mean to you?
(See Appendix B, page 107.)

4. Who encourages you to seek first the kingdom of God in your health situation? (Matt. 6:33)

   a. Who or what interferes with your search for increased intimacy with God?

   b. Whom do you encourage to pursue Godly intimacy?

Scripture Passage: 2 Cor. 5:11-21 NIV

5. Because Jesus died for your sins, what is your appropriate response to Him? (v. 15)

   a. List three ways you live for Christ:
   ➢
   ➢

b. Did your list include activities or relationships?

c. How do health conditions hinder your activities and complicate your relationships?

6. What happens to you spiritually when you are in Christ? (v. 17) (See Appendix B, page 107.)

    a. What is your *old*?

    b. What is your *new*?

Memory Verse: "*For God so loved the world that he gave his one and only Son, that whoever believes in him shall not perish but have eternal life.*" (John 3:16 NIV) (See Appendix A, pages 90-94.)

Today's Challenge:

1. How will you cope?

2. What will be your attitude?

Prayer Partner's needs:

➤

➤

In Jesus' Name: (activities for a good day)

1. Spend time with a friend who is waiting for medical test results.

2. Make and share your favorite dessert with someone you love.

3. Create a meaningful bookmark, coaster, or plaque that will remind you of how blessed you are.

STUDY 2: *Where will I find my Savior?*

Jesus said, *"I-AM the door: by me if any man enter in, he shall be saved..."* (John 10:9a KJV)

Being *saved* is common Christian vernacular describing people who believe in Jesus Christ and ask to receive Him into their lives. Jesus is our I-AM God and is the open door to relationship with God. He declares, *"Here I am! I stand at the door and knock. If anyone hears my voice and opens the door, I will come in and eat with him, and he with me."* (Rev. 3:20 NIV) God has provided for our spiritual well-being when we go through the door to Christ.

1. What does the word "salvation" mean to you?
   (See Appendix B, page 108.)

2. How does your relationship with Christ energize and give you hope? If it doesn't, why not?

Scripture Passage: John 10:7-18 NIV

3. What are some characteristics of sheep?
   (See Appendix B, page 108.)

a. Can you identify and explain any sheep behavior in yourself?

b. What did Jesus do for His sheep? (v. 9, 10, 15)

c. What does Jesus do for His wounded sheep?

4. Jesus declares that the Jewish leaders are thieves and hired hands who do not have the best interest of God's people at heart.

   a. What does the thief come to do? (v. 10)

   b. What does the hired hand do when trouble comes? (v. 12-13)

   c. What does a good shepherd do? (v. 11, 14)

   d. Why does Jesus come for His sheep? (v. 10)

5. What choice did God give Jesus Christ concerning His life? (v. 17-18)

a. What options do you see available to you in your circumstances and health situation?

b. What choices do you have with respect to your relationships?

6. Do you ever feel as if you have failed God? How would He respond to that attitude? (Phil. 3:8-9)
(See Appendix B, page 108.)

Memory Verse: *"For God so loved the world that he gave his one and only Son, that whoever believes in him shall not perish but have eternal life."* (John 3:16 NIV) (See Appendix A, pages 90-94.)

Today's Challenge:

1. How will you cope?

2. What will be your attitude?

Prayer Partner's needs:

➤

➤

In Jesus' Name: (activities for a good day)

1. Think of some of your favorite hymns or songs. Make a short list and put it in a place you will remember. When you're dragging your feet and can't get motivated, check your list and sing the happiest tunes you know.

2. Rearrange several pieces of furniture to give you a fresh perspective on your circumstances.

3. Baby-sit for a harried friend, family or church member who does not have much time to relax, even if it's just for half-an-hour.

4. Make sure that all your friends' and family's birthdays are listed on your calendar. If you don't know someone's date, call and ask.

5. Offer to write or type a letter for a person whose finger mobility makes writing a difficult task.

6. Clip out cartoons from the newspaper and send or email them to friends and family.

STUDY 3: *Who is my Savior?*

"Looking for that blessed hope, and the glorious appearing of the great God and our Saviour Jesus Christ; Who gave himself for us, that he might redeem us from all iniquity, and purify unto himself a peculiar people, zealous of good works." (Titus 2:13-14 KJV)

God chose Abraham to father a nation that would bless all the people of the earth. He selected the nation of Israel: *"For you are a people holy to the LORD your God. The LORD your God has chosen you out of all the peoples on the face of the earth to be his people, his treasured possession. The LORD did not set his affection on you and choose you because you were more numerous than other peoples, for you were the fewest of all peoples. But it was because the LORD loved you and kept the oath he swore to your forefathers that he brought you out with a mighty hand and redeemed you from the land of slavery, from the power of Pharaoh king of Egypt."* (Deut. 7:6-8 NIV) God chose the Jews, not because they were better than any other nationality, but because through them the Savior, the Messiah, would come. Israel was to declare this good news of salvation to all the nations of the world. (Gen. 12:2-3)

1. What kind of *peculiar* Christian are you?
(See Appendix B, page 109.)

2. Define *zeal* in your own words. (See Appendix B, page 109.)

3. Define *good works*. (See Appendix B, page 109.)

4. When do you feel zealous to do a good work?

    a. Who decides what your good work will be? (Eph. 2:10)

    b. For whom do you do good works? (Col. 3:23-24)

    c. Who begins and completes your good work? (Phil. 1:16)

    d. If God ordains your good works, how can your chronic condition interfere?

Scripture Passage: Titus 2:1-15 NIV

5. Which behaviors, described in verses 2-8, are relevant to you? Why?

6. In Galatians, Paul clarifies the relationship Jesus Christ the Messiah has with the Jewish nation. He also addresses the behaviors you listed in question five:

"We Jews know that we have no advantage of birth over 'non-Jewish sinners.' We know very well that we are not set right with God by rule keeping but only through personal faith in Jesus Christ. How do we know? We tried it—and we had the best system of rules the world has ever seen! Convinced that no human being can please God by self-improvement, we believed in Jesus as the Messiah so that we might be set right before God by trusting in the Messiah, not by trying to be good. Have some of you noticed that we are not yet perfect? (No great surprise, right?)... What actually took place is this: I tried keeping rules and working my head off to please God, and it didn't work. So I quit being a 'law man' so that I could be God's man. Christ's life showed me how, and enabled me to do it. I identified myself completely with him... Christ lives in me. The life you see me living is not 'mine,' but it is lived by faith in the Son of God, who loved me and gave himself for me." (Gal. 2:15-20 Msg)

The law Paul refers to is the Law of Moses, including the Ten Commandments. (Reread this passage in a study Bible such as the NIV for a more accurate translation.)
(See Appendix B, page 109.)

 a. What was Paul's, or any Jew's, success in following the Law?

 b. How did Paul become *God's man*?

c. Are you God's man or woman? Explain.

Memory Verse: *"For God so loved the world that he gave his one and only Son, that whoever believes in him shall not perish but have eternal life."* (John 3:16 NIV) (See Appendix A, pages 90-94.)

Today's Challenge:

1. How will you cope?

2. What will be your attitude?

Prayer Partner's needs:

➤

➤

In Jesus' Name: (See pages 29 or 69.)

61
Chapter Three

STUDY 4: *How does my Savior save me?*

"The next day John saw Jesus coming toward him and said, 'Look! There is the Lamb of God who takes away the sin of the world!'" (John 1:29 NLT)

While the Jews waited for their conquering Messiah, they followed the Law of Moses that required an unblemished lamb to be sacrificed every year to take away their sins for that year. (Lev. 14:12-13) Sin kept them, as it keeps us today, separated from God. John the Baptist witnessed that Jesus Christ was the Son of God, Messiah in the flesh. Jesus would be the last sacrificial lamb whose blood would allow all believers to have unhindered fellowship with God at last.

1. John the Baptist was famous in his day for rebuking the Jewish people for their sins and baptizing those who repented. Jewish tradition required only Gentile converts be baptized. John's ministry was a novelty.

    a. What did John call Jesus?

    b. How could he know about the purpose of Jesus' life?

    c. What was that purpose?

2. Since perfect Jesus was sacrificed for **all** of your sins, there no longer needs to be a perfect you. In light of this truth, what expectations of perfection would you like to let go? (See Appendix B, page 110.)

Scripture Passage: John 1:19-34 NIV

3. Who did Jewish leaders send to question John? (v. 19, 24)

4. John's life had a message and a purpose. What were they?

    a. Message (v. 29)

    b. Purpose (v. 31)

5. Has God given you a message and a purpose?

    a. If so, what are they?

    b. If not, whose counsel could you seek?

6. The word "Trinity" is not used in the Bible, though we find it used elsewhere in song lyrics, scholarly studies, and sermons. (See Appendix B, page 110.)

   a. What does the phrase, "Holy Trinity," mean to you?

   b. Read Matt. 28:18-20. Jesus Himself identifies the Trinity. Who *is* God?

Memory Verse: *"For God so loved the world that he gave his one and only Son, that whoever believes in him shall not perish but have eternal life."* (John 3:16 NIV) (See Appendix A, pages 90-94.)

Today's Challenge:

1. How will you cope?

2. What will be your attitude?

Prayer Partner's needs:

➢

➢

In Jesus' Name: (activities for a good day)

1. Collect gift-wrapping supplies throughout the year. Visit a friend who is housebound or in a healthcare facility. Share your materials, and help him or her gift-wrap items or make a collage together.

2. Pray before your next visit to the doctors that God will put in your path medical personnel who need to know the good news of Jesus Christ. Remember, He will equip you for this "window of opportunity."

3. Have friends come over for a card game, dominoes, or a TV special when you're feeling out of sorts. Set a time limit on the activity so you don't overdo it.

4. *"Do not let any unwholesome talk come out of your mouths, but only what is helpful for building others up according to their needs..."* (Eph. 4:29 NIV) Make a list of positive attributes for someone who is in a personal identity crisis. Share your list in person, in a card, through an email, or on the phone.

STUDY 5: *Why do I have a Savior?*

"For God so loved the world that he gave his only Son, so that everyone who believes in him will not perish but have eternal life. God did not send his Son into the world to condemn it, but to save it." (John 3:16-17 NLT)

God beckons to us with arms open wide. He loves every soul upon this earth, and He desires that all come to know His Son, Jesus Christ. As Christians, we are called to that same all-encompassing love for each other, even for the ugly, the undeserving, and the unlikable. This love is only possible through the power of Jesus' love in our life.

1. Why did God send Jesus Christ to earth?

2. Who have you condemned in thought or action? Explain how you can adjust your attitude concerning him or her.

3. Whom do you know that needs to hear the good news about Jesus Christ? (See Appendix B, page 111.)

   a. What circumstances would be conducive to bringing up the subject of having a personal relationship with Jesus Christ?

b. What would you say?

Scripture Passage: John 3:1-21 NIV

4. To what did Jesus compare being born again? (v. 8)

5. Would you have been exasperated with Nicodemus, a leader in the synagogue? Was Jesus? (v. 10-12) Explain your answer.

   a. What exasperates you about your health condition?

   b. Write or say a quick prayer asking Jesus to give you peace when health situations seem insurmountable.

6. Jesus is compared to light. (v. 19-21)

   a. How can people reject God's light?

   b. Who comes to the light?

c. What can be plainly seen in the light?

7. In Ps. 36 of *The Message*, it states: "*You're a fountain of cascading light, and you open our eyes to light.*" (Ps. 36:9 Msg) Draw what this verbal picture looks like to you.

Memory Verse: "For God so loved the world that he gave his one and only Son, that whoever believes in him shall not perish but have eternal life." (John 3:16 NIV) (See Appendix A, pages 90-94.)

Today's Challenge:

1. How will you cope?

2. What will be your attitude?

Prayer Partner's needs:

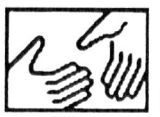

➢

➢

In Jesus' Name: (activities for a good day)

1. Pet-sit for a friend or get involved with a local animal adoption agency in your area.

2. Pick out two identical items—rocks, dime store rings, empty rolls of toilet paper, etc. Put your name on one and your friend's name on the other. Each of you place the item in a frequently used part of the house or office. When you glance at the item, say a short prayer for your friend, as he or she will for you.

3. Take a string of Christmas tree lights with you when you visit a shut-in, a person hospitalized, or a nursing home resident. String the lights around the room or around the TV. May the lights be a remembrance of your visit and a reminder that Jesus lightens one's burdens.

4. Make or buy cute refrigerator magnets that will make you smile and remind you to pray for someone in need.

CHAPTER FOUR

God affirms that Jesus is the way to Him.

The solution to mankind's dilemma—sin separating us from God—is found in Jesus' statement, *"No one comes to the Father except through me."* (John 14:6 NIV) Jesus is stating that the presence of God in our lives occurs only when we believe that *He* is the I-AM whom Moses met at the burning bush. Jesus declares He existed before creation, He is now with His creation—that's us—and He will be with us through all eternity. He existed before our pain, is with us now in our pain, and will be there when our pain is no more.

We want to get at truth by "shortcuts"; the wonder is our Lord's amazing patience. He never insists that we take His way; He simply says, "I am the way." We might as well learn to take His way at the beginning, but we won't, we are determined on our own way.

Oswald Chambers, *The Place of Help*, 1935.

STUDY 1: *Jesus is the Way.*

"Jesus told him, 'I am the way, the truth, and the life. No one comes to the Father except through Me.'"
(John 14:6 HCSB)

Jesus proclaims: I-AM your *Way*! I-AM your *Truth*! I-AM your *Life*! He virtually draws a line in the sand. We either believe He is God in the flesh or we do not. Jesus declares He is our only access to Holy God; and we can look to the Bible to confirm this truth. The Bible is not a menu from which we choose the parts we agree with and ignore the rest. To accept the Bible as God's infallible word is to accept with certainty that Jesus is who He says He is.

1. Is your heart settled that Father God, Jesus Christ the Son, and the Holy Spirit *is* God? Explain why. If not, what questions do you still have that need answers?
(See Appendix B, page 112.)

2. Many people have trouble accepting the exclusiveness of this Scripture. How might you respond to someone who does not agree that Jesus is the *only* way?
(See Appendix B, page 112-113.)

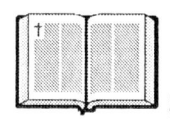

Scripture Passage: John 14:1-14 NIV

3. Is your heart sometimes troubled? What does Scripture tell you to do when upsetting feelings occur? (v. 1)

4. Verse two in the King James reads, "*In my Father's house are many mansions: if it were not so, I would have told you. I go to prepare a place for you.*" (John 14:2 KJV)

   a. Describe the magnificent mansion God is building for you.

   b. What must you do to receive this mansion? (v. 6)

5. List the top three concerns for which you would like answers:

   ➤

   ➤

   ➤

   a. Does it feel as if God is withholding answers for these concerns?

b. Why would God withhold answers to your prayers?

c. Would foresight make your life easier? Why or why not?

6. By studying Jesus' teachings, what three scriptural applications have been helpful in living with your chronic condition? (v. 7-14)

➤

➤

➤

Memory Verse: *"Jesus answered, 'I am the way and the truth and the life. No one comes to the Father except through me.'"* (John 14:6 NIV)
(See Appendix A, pages 90-94.)

Today's Challenge:

1. How will you cope?

2. What will be your attitude?

Prayer Partner's needs:

➢

➢

In Jesus' Name: (activities for a good day)

1. Offer a busy mom or over-extended dad your willingness to mail their packages or pick up stamps when you go to the post office.

2. Find a bright poster that cheers you up just looking at it. Display it where others can enjoy it too.

3. Reflect on what books have helped you with your chronic condition and make a list. Reread the most helpful books again, and offer your list to someone else who is in pain.

4. Trade spaces with someone who has a different chronic illness—just for an hour. Share insights.

5. Take someone's children to Sunday School when they are ill.

STUDY 2: *Jesus is the Light.*

"As long as I am in the world, I am the light of the world." (John 9:5 HCSB)

The Apostle John portrays Jesus as light; and men who live in darkness flee (John 1:4-5) because this light exposes all men to the truth (John 3:21). Jesus' light gives men eternal life (John 8:12) and assures them that they will never again live in darkness (John 12:46). These portrayals were prophesized by Isaiah in the Old Testament. (Isa. 49:6, 60:1-3) He declared that the Messiah would restore the nation of Israel, and would be the light of salvation to the Gentiles.

1. Can you remember a situation where God's light seemed to be missing, such as: an argument, a discourtesy, an indiscretion, or a thoughtless response? Explain how Jesus' presence would have, or did, make a difference.

2. What does the word *grace* mean to you?
   (See Appendix B, page 113.)

   a. In what circumstances do you see God's grace?

   b. What situations seem to be devoid of His grace?

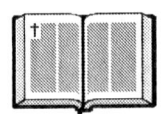

Scripture Passage: John 9:1-34 NIV

3. Why was this man born blind? (v. 3)

4. From your experience with Bible stories and Scripture study, was any other person ever healed by spit and mud? (v. 6-7)

   a. What different methods did Jesus use to heal people? (See Appendix B, page 113.)

   b. Read John 5:2-5. Out of the "great multitude," Jesus healed one person. He could have healed them all. Why do you think He didn't?

   c. What are some positive reasons Jesus might have to keep from healing you at this time?

5. Why were the Pharisees upset with Jesus? (v. 13-16)

6. Which would be more important to the blind man—healing for his blindness or good standing with the Jewish community? Why?

   a. What were the Jewish leaders thinking? (v. 28-29, 34)

   b. What was the attitude of the healed man? (v. 30-31)

   c. Share a time in your life when you could echo the blind man's words: "I was blind but now I see." (v. 25)

Memory Verse: *"Jesus answered, 'I am the way and the truth and the life. No one comes to the Father except through me.'"* (John 14:6 NIV)
(See Appendix A, pages 90-94.)

Today's Challenge:

1. How will you cope?

2. What will be your attitude?

Prayer Partner's needs:

➢

➢

In Jesus' Name: (activities for a good day)

1. Phone, write, or email someone who has encouraged you. Use words such as: *bolster, boost, cheer up, gladden, hearten, inspire, reassure, relieve, soothe, support,* and *up-lift.*

2. Put pictures together of a special event and share them with someone who couldn't go.

3. Offer to clean the shower stall or tub for a hurting friend.

4. Design an encouragement bulletin board and tack up items that have boosted your morale, gladdened your heart, and cheered you up. Examine your board often, especially when you need an attitude adjustment.

STUDY 3: *Jesus is the Bread of Life.*

"*Jesus replied, 'I-AM the Bread of Life. He who comes to Me will never be hungry, and he who believes in and cleaves to and trusts in and relies on Me will never thirst any more (at any time).'*" (John 6:35 AB)

Jesus made this controversial statement the day after He miraculously fed five thousand people with two small fish and five small loaves of barley bread. (John 6:1-15) His previous recipients sought Him out the next day so that He could feed them again. But Jesus declared that He was the imperishable bread. All people should feast upon Him: through His kingdom on earth as it is in heaven (Matt. 6:10), through His communion (1 Cor. 11:23-24), and through His church (Eph. 1:22-23). When Jesus declared He was living bread, many people no longer followed Him. His statement winnowed the people who had a heart for God from those who followed Jesus with curiosity, for free food, or for the novelty. (John 6:60-66)

1. Bread was the food of survival in Bible times. In what area of your life is Jesus crucial?

2. Do pain medications interfere with your *believing, cleaving, trusting,* and *relying* on Jesus Christ?

    a. Explain when medications interfere with your *believing, cleaving, trusting,* and *relying*.

    b. Share or brainstorm with someone what you can do to minimize these hurdles.

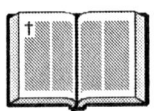

Scripture Passage: John 6:25-51 NIV

3. What kind of food endures for eternal life? (v. 27)

4. What work must you do to receive God's bread of life? (v. 28-29) (See Appendix B, page 113.)

   a. Will doing church activities or church ministry give you eternal life? Explain your answer.

   b. Will your chronic condition impede the work God is asking of you? Explain.

5. The Jews of Jesus' day were mistakenly attributing Moses with providing manna in the wilderness. (v. 30-31, 49)

   a. Who provided manna for the survival of Israel during forty years of wandering? (v. 32)

   b. What is the difference between the manna God provided through Moses when the Jews were in the wilderness and His provision for us of the living bread of life through Jesus Christ? (v. 33, 49-51)

6. Why did Jesus come to earth and what did He give you as a result? (v. 39, 40, 47)

Memory Verse: "*Jesus answered, 'I am the way and the truth and the life. No one comes to the Father except through me.'*" (John 14:6 NIV)
(See Appendix A, pages 90-94.)

Today's Challenge:

1. How will you cope?

2. What will be your attitude?

Prayer Partner's needs:

➤

➤

In Jesus' Name: (activities for a good day)

1. Organize your clothes closet by seasons.

2. Have an all night adult sleepover: pop popcorn, shoot hoops, do puzzles, manicure each other's toenails, share jokes or sport stories, do finger painting with chocolate pudding, try out a new hair color, watch movies, sing karaoke, and share war stories.

3. Make a cover for a blank journal that says: *My fantasy for you is...* Give it to a sick friend and provide colorful marking pens. When visitors come calling, they will be able to write encouraging messages or draw funny pictures for your friend.

4. Discover an unwell friend's favorite toy as a child. Because illness can make one feel so old, try to find a similar item and give it to him or her as a special gift.

5. Send an up-beat note or email to a friend when **you** are feeling blue.

STUDY 4: *Jesus is the Vine.*

Jesus said, *"I am the vine, you are the branches; he who abides in Me, and I in him, he bears much fruit; for apart from Me you can do nothing."* (John 15:5 NASB)

Wine was a common beverage in Biblical times just as it is today. By using the grapevine as a spiritual metaphor, Jesus illustrates our dependency on Him. He is the trunk of the plant, and nourishment for the branches must come through Him. The grapes represent the good works God has planned for us to do and are only possible through the provision of the trunk. Picture Jesus as a healthy grapevine trunk and yourself as one of His branches. What size are you? How green are your leaves? How are your bunches of grapes coming along? How much of Jesus is in the vine? How much of Jesus is in you, His branch?

1. Carefully consider the questions above then draw Jesus as the grapevine trunk and you as one of His branches with leaves and fruit.

2. From whom does your fruit originate? (See Appendix B, page 114.)

    a. Who is responsible for the health and quantity of your fruit?

b. How does your chronic health condition affect the maturation of leaves and grapes growing on your branch?

c. Do you have to be physically healthy to be fruitful for Jesus? Explain your answer.

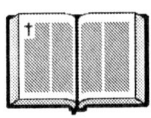

Scripture Passage: John 15:1-17 NIV

3. What happens to branches that:

   a. bear no fruit? (v. 2, 6)

   b. bear fruit? (v. 2, 7, 8)

4. What does Jesus command in verse twelve?

   a. What does Jesus' love look like? (v. 13)

   b. What does your love look like on good days?

c. How does your love appear on bad days?

5. Does verse sixteen mean that if you ask for good health you will automatically get it? If yes, why? If no, why not?

   a. Have you ever thought that if you just had enough faith you would be healed? Who ensures your healing in this scenario, you or Jesus?

   b. Paul asks the Galatians the same question: *"Let me ask you this one question: Did you receive the Holy Spirit by keeping the law? Of course not, for the Holy Spirit came upon you only after you believed the message you heard about Christ. Have you lost your senses? After starting your Christian lives in the Spirit, why are you now trying to become perfect by your own human effort?"* (Gal.3:2-3 NLT) How would you answer his question?

6. Consider your greatest struggle.

   a. Explain whether you need more head knowledge or heart knowing to deal with this challenge.

b. Does the knowledge of God's promises make a difference in your day-to-day living? Why or why not?

Memory Verse: *"Jesus answered, 'I am the way and the truth and the life. No one comes to the Father except through me.'"* (John 14:6 NIV)
(See Appendix A, pages 90-94.)

Today's Challenge:

1. How will you cope?

2. What will be your attitude?

Prayer Partner's needs:

➢

➢

In Jesus' Name: (see page 34.)

STUDY 5: *Jesus is the Resurrection.*

"Jesus said to her, 'I am the resurrection and the life. He who believes in me will live, even though he dies; and whoever lives and believes in me will never die. Do you believe this?'" (John 11:25-26 NIV)

Sin causes spiritual separation from God. Restoration from sin only comes through Jesus Christ. Our belief in Jesus brings us immediately into the kingdom of God. We may choose Jesus as our life, or we may choose sin as a living death. Sometimes, as in this story of Mary, Martha and Lazarus, Jesus raises a physically dead body back to life. Even today, He may heal miraculously; but Jesus said, *"The Spirit gives life; the flesh counts for nothing. The words I have spoken to you are spirit and they are life."* (John 6:63 NIV) So it is our souls that concern Him most since these earthly bodies are not heaven-bound.

1. Define *resurrection* in your own words.
(See Appendix B, page 114.)

2. Jesus is the resurrection and the _____. How does your resurrection by Jesus occur?

3. God encourages you to trust Him through this present time of suffering. On a scale of 1-10, what does your trust look like right now? Why?

a. If your faith and trust need only be the size of a mustard seed (Matt. 17:20), is God disappointed in your score? (See Appendix B, page 115.)

b. How can you be discouraged when God is not?

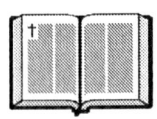

Scripture Passage: John 11:1-44 NIV

4. Why did Jesus allow Lazarus to die? (v. 4, 14, 41-42)

5. Choose one of the characters in this story: Mary, Martha, a disciple, a mourner, the rock remover, or Lazarus.

   a. What concerns would this person have while Lazarus was still alive?

   b. What thoughts could your character have had once Lazarus died?

   c. What emotions would your person have felt as Lazarus walked out of the tomb?

6. What circumstances or relationships has God used to teach you more about Himself?

Memory Verse: *"Jesus answered, 'I am the way and the truth and the life. No one comes to the Father except through me.'"* (John 14:6 NIV)
(See Appendix A, pages 90-94.)

Today's Challenge:

1. How will you cope?

2. What will be your attitude?

Prayer Partner's needs:

➤

➤

APPENDIX A

Memorizing Scripture

Memorizing Scripture satisfies one's hunger to meditate upon God's words day and night. (Ps. 1:2) As a person with chronic pain, however, memorizing can be stressful. The Old Testament states that through discipline and study there is a reward: *"Do not let this Book of the Law depart from your mouth; meditate on it day and night, so that you may be careful to do everything written in it. Then you will be prosperous and successful."* (Josh. 1:8 NIV) Try using **a key, a commitment, a plan,** and **accountability,** to empower your study and memory of God's words.

THE KEY? *Holy Spirit Power!*

Invite the Holy Spirit to divinely enable you to learn God's life-changing words. Confess God's ability to plant His words, not just in your mind, but in your heart as well: *"May the God of hope fill you with all joy and peace as you trust in him, so that you may overflow with hope by the power of the Holy Spirit."* (Rom. 15:13 NIV)

THE COMMITMENT? *Daily Effort!*

Make a decision to prepare yourself with God's truth so that you can meet over-whelming circumstances and distressing relationships with God's words: *"...the one [Holy Spirit] who is in you is greater than the one [Satan] who is in the world."* (1 John 4:4b NIV)

THE PLAN? *Consistency With The Details!*

Decide <u>why</u> you want to memorize Scripture. Then determine <u>how</u> long you want to study the verse, be it two minutes or ten, just make the commitment. <u>Where</u> will you practice the verse? <u>What</u> materials will you need? <u>When</u> will you practice?

The habit of hiding God's word in your heart may come more quickly if you add it to something you already do daily. If Bible study is an everyday occurrence, add five minutes of memorizing. If quiet time with the Lord is sporadic or often interrupted, don't despair.

    a. Brush your teeth daily? Add 5 minutes of study.
    b. Commuting a grind? Tape record the verse or carry a 3x5 card with the verse on it while in transit.
    c. Picking up kids? Arrive early so that you can practice your verse.
    d. Read before going to sleep? Add pencil and paper to the nightstand.
    e. Have a daily constitutional? Place memorizing materials within easy reach.

Planning is essential to successfully memorizing Scripture: "*Suppose one of you wants to build a tower. Will he not first sit down and estimate the cost to see if he has enough money to complete it?*" (Luke 14:28 NIV) Try using each of the following techniques to determine which methods are effective for you.

1. Say, then copy the memory verse for each chapter in your journal, on a 3x5 card, or in this workbook. Place the Scripture reference at the beginning and at the end like this:

John 1:18. *"No one has ever seen God, but God the One and Only, who is at the Father's side, has made him known."* John 1:18.

Check to make sure you have placed words in the exact order and punctuation is accurate. You will want to refer back to your written verse each day. Use a Bible dictionary or glossary—frequently found in the back of your Bible—to look up any unfamiliar words.

2. Write or say a personal gratitude prayer based on the Scripture. For John 1:18, it might go something like this: "Father God, I am so thankful that you sent your One and Only—Jesus Christ—to give me a glimmer of who you are and how much you love me. The life, death, and resurrection of Jesus reveals your passion for fellowship with me."

3. Restate the verse in your own words, applying it directly to yourself, such as: "John 1:18. Only Jesus has seen Father God because He was, is, and shall always be by His side; and when I die I too shall see God on His throne. John 1:18."

4. Say, then write the verse. Check to make sure it is totally accurate. Look for patterns in punctuation and phrasing (P&P), first letter and word patterns (L&W), and look for any gimmick to help you remember ☺. For example in John 1:18:

   a. Punctuation and phrasing (P&P)—there are three commas making four phrases to learn.

   b. Letter and word patterns (L&W)—*"God, but God"* (word pattern), *"One and Only"* (letter pattern), *"has seen"* and *"has made"* (verbs).

c. Gimmicks ☺—fun stuff that helps you laugh, dance, sing, or draw while you learn. In the Scripture example, John 1:18, there are two ones in the address and the second word of the verse is also one. This gimmick might make you smile: "John one-and-a-one-and-an-eight-and-a-No-one" (John 1:18 "*No one has ever seen God...*").

5. Draw pictures for some of the words or use different colored pens. Try writing Scripture verses with chalk or paint. Use sand, rice, or chocolate pudding as your method and have fun cleaning up ☺. You might try singing your verse. (Scripture put to music can be found at: www.joycenter.on.ca/menujs.hl?cass4.h)

6. Say, then copy the verse leaving out important words, like this:

_____ 1:18 "_____ _____ has ever seen _____, but _____ the _____ and _____, who is at _____ _____, has made _____ _____." John _____

Rewrite the verse filling in the missing words. Then, say or write the verse again without looking.

7. Share your memory verse with email friends by typing it again and again for each friend instead of copying and pasting the text.

Choose the methods useful to you and don't fret. Scientists have determined that you learn more from your mistakes then you do when you don't make any.

ACCOUNTABILITY? *Stifle Procrastination!*

Commit reciting your Scripture memory verse to at least one person each week.. *"Though one may be overpowered, two can defend themselves. A cord of three strands is not quickly broken."* (Eccl. 4:12 NIV)

You will never regret accessing Holy Spirit power, committing to daily effort, planning for consistency, and requiring accountability in learning God's words. It is not the speed or quantity of verses learned that is crucial, but rather keeping spiritually healthy with God's words deep in your heart for the tough times in life. *"Love the LORD your God with all your heart and with all your soul and with all your strength. These commandments that I give you today are to be upon your hearts..."* (Deut. 6:5-6 NIV)

APPENDIX B

Reader's Guide

Jesus spoke to His disciples and followers, saying, *"But among you* [fellow believers], *those who are the greatest should take the lowest rank, and the leader should be like a servant."* (Luke 22:26 NLT)

Living with a chronic condition is certainly a challenge. Sometimes it's easy to forget that the glass is half full rather than half empty. A support group helps keep our lives in perspective. It also provides us with accountability for replacing crippling habits with Scripture-based solutions. Sharing trials and victories in a group setting sparks recognition that God is interested in the minutiae of our every day living. Our pain is neither arbitrary nor punishment. It's an opportunity to enhance our fellowship with Jesus Christ.

Leader's study options:

- Decide if the study lessons will be homework prior to the group meeting, completed at the Bible study itself, or will be done as a follow-up to your get-together.

- Determine if you will meet every week, every other week, or once a month.

- If pressed for time, consider combining some of the studies or omitting some of the questions inapplicable to your group.

Leader's preparation before the group meets:

- Do the study yourself. Choose questions that are relevant to the needs of your group, and make sure these are discussed.

- Make a list of members' names, phone numbers, email and home addresses. If you have permission from each member, make copies for everyone.

- Take advantage of your own support group and/or prayer partners to help you pray for the struggles, the needs, and the comfort of each group member.

- Prepare in advance the materials, props, or room arrangement you will need to encourage participation.

- Come up with ideas for skits, songs, and artwork if you are creative.

- Never "cancel" a meeting. Always "reschedule!"

Leader's activities during the Bible study:

- Start on time and open in prayer.

- Plan time for one member of the group to share his or her testimony. At the first meeting, pass around a sign-up sheet on which each person can choose a date. Use the list to call or to send a postcard as a timely reminder when it's each person's turn.

- Discuss the praises and difficulties associated with having prayer partners. Brainstorm possible solutions.

- Review with the group the insights and the commitments made at the last meeting, and talk over the participants' follow-through.

- Take notes throughout the current meeting on any insights and commitments made while discussing the Bible text and questions—these notes will assist with follow-up for the next meeting.

- Draw new prayer partners and discuss their immediate needs.

- Close in prayer.

CHAPTER ONE: *God declares Jesus is His Son.*

📖 Leader, give your testimony at the first meeting.

📖 Familiarize yourself with the organization of this devotional Bible study by reviewing the section "How To Use This Study" on pages 7-9.

STUDY 1: *Who is Jesus?* (Chap. 1)

📖 Jesus and God have the same name.

📖 Background: Jewish leaders in the synagogue were the base of power during the time of Jesus. These leaders were composed of: the *scribes,* who were considered the experts in Biblical interpretation; the *Pharisees,* who believed that Torah—the man-made oral and written interpretations of the law—was equal with the God-given Law of Moses; and the *Sadducees,* who scrupulously followed the letter of the law, but not its underlying principles. The synagogue was the focal point of daily Jewish living. Every Jewish man, woman, and child was impacted by the events occurring in the synagogue.

The Romans occupied and ruled the nation of Israel, but everything Roman was abhorred and shunned by the Jewish community. The Jewish leaders in power had to maneuver within the political confines of Roman occupation and still appear to scrupulously follow the laws and oral traditions of their religion and way of life.

Question 2: *Easton's Illustrated Dictionary* clarifies the Biblical term of *blasphemy*: "In the sense of speaking evil of God this word is found in (Ps 74:18; Isa 52:5; Rom 2:24; Rev 13:1, 6; Rev 16:9, 11, 21). It denotes also any kind of calumny, or evil-speaking, or abuse (1Ki 21:10; Acts 13:45; Acts 18:6). Our Lord was accused of blasphemy when he claimed to be the Son of God (Mat 26:65; Compare Mat 9:3; Mark 2:7). They who deny his Messiahship blaspheme Jesus (Luke 22:65; John 10:36)."

Stoning was the capital punishment for blasphemy and was prescribed in the Law of Moses, Lev. 24:14-16.

Question 3: Refer to 2 Chron. 20:17, Matt. 6:25-34, and 2 Cor. 9:8.

Question 7: Many people pick and choose what they want to believe regarding the Bible and Jesus Christ. To be a Christian, one must commit whole-heartedly to two truths: Jesus **is** God, and the Bible **is** the inerrant word of God.

Leader, try to discern who in the group is having difficulty with these two beliefs. Insert and imply throughout your time together the Gospel message:

1. God loves us. (John 3:16)
2. All of us have sinned. (Rom. 3:23)
3. Jesus died for our sins. (Rom. 5:8)
4. We must invite Jesus into our hearts. (Rev. 3:20)

Memory Verse: Review Appendix A, pages 90-94, and discuss the importance of learning God's words. Decide how memorizing Scripture can be accomplished within the confines of your chronic condition.

Prayer Partners: Leader, have each participant put their name and phone number on a 3x5 card. Mix the cards, then have each draw the name of someone for whom they will pray. Discuss the commitment of praying for their partner and making contact at least once before the next meeting. If you are doing the study by yourself, ask a friend to partner with you in prayer. Pray for each other at least once a week.

STUDY 2: *Why did Jesus come to Earth?* (Chap. 1)

Jesus' time on earth was to reveal and make known who God is.

Question 1: This Amplified Bible version of John 1:18 is chosen as the devotional verse of Study 2 as it provides the practice on how decipher difficult Bible passages by identifying who is speaking and to whom the pronouns are referring. John 1:18 is stated in the NIV version of the Bible as: *"No one has ever seen God, but God the One and Only, who is at the Father's side, has made him known."*

The rewrite of the Amplified Bible translation is: *"No man has ever seen God at any time; the only unique Son, or the only begotten God, Who is in the bosom [in the intimate Presence] of the Father,* **Christ** *has declared* **the Father** *[Christ has revealed* **the Father** *and brought* **the Father** *out where* **the Father** *can be seen;* **Christ** *has interpreted* **the Father** *and* **Christ** *has made* **the Father** *known]."* (John 1:18 AB)

Question 5: God's law was given to the nation of Israel through Moses. This law specified sinful behavior that required repentance. The yearly sacrificial lamb was a cleansing for the Jews so that they could again have fellowship with God. By the time of Jesus, however, Jewish leadership was no longer guiding the people to worship God through the Law of Moses, but rather to worship the Law itself. Thus they did not recognize Jesus Christ as God's answer for eternal forgiveness of sin. Rom. 8:1-2 and Rom. 7:14-25 address the issue of Law vs. Spirit.

STUDY 3: *What did Jesus' works reveal?* (Chap. 1)

Jesus is in the Father and the Father is in Jesus.

Question 1: Read Matt. 8:23-27, Mark 5:21-43, and John 9:1-41. These were just three of the many miracles Jesus performed.

Question 2: When God calls us to do His good works—feeding the hungry, worshipping, preaching, evangelizing, and teaching—we have a successful, fulfilling, effective ministry in God's kingdom. Man's good works may look the same by outward appearance, but the motivating factors are all about *shoulds*—we should feed the hungry, we should worship, we should preach, evangelize, and teach. When performing out of man's efforts, the shoulds can lead to guilt, misdirected energy, and burn-out.

STUDY 4: *Is Jesus separate from Father God?*
(Chap. 1)

📖 What God can do, Jesus did, does, and will do.

📖 Question 1: Even with our advanced technology and modern breakthroughs, we cannot cure leprosy, only treat it. We cannot walk on water nor raise the dead after four days. God can. Jesus did.

📖 Question 5: Do you ask God for more things, better relationships, or changed circumstances? How do these requests compare with God's will for your life?

📖 Question 6: God will always respond to the name of Jesus; but His answer to your need—yes, no or wait—may not be what you expect.

STUDY 5: *How can a man be God?* (Chap. 1)

📖 God determined that He would appear to His creation as a man. We accept this by faith.

📖 Question 3: The first criminal hardened his heart and mocked God. The second criminal opened his heart, was forgiven, and received a divine promise. You have these same heart choices regarding your circumstances. Ask God where your heart is hardened and pray for a changed attitude so that you receive divine blessings.

📖 In Jesus Name #4: Leader, assign each member of your group one the line of the Scripture to rewrite and apply.

CHAPTER TWO: God identifies Jesus with many names.

📱 Leader, begin the group meeting by discussing the meaning of the participant's name or the names in their family. It would be interesting to have a book on naming babies if it gives the meaning and origin of various names.

STUDY 1: *Jesus is the cornerstone.* (Chap. 2)

📱 Background: Jesus is the foundation of all churches, no matter what denomination, when they declare He is the Son of God who died for people's sins. Church attendance and good works do not make one a Christian. A personal relationship with Jesus Christ, through believing and receiving Him into one's life, is the only way.

📱 Leader, assess your group members. Do they need to hear the Gospel every session? Partner non-believers with the stronger believers in your group who have confessed that Jesus Christ is Lord.

STUDY 2: *Jesus is the church.* (Chap. 2)

📱 Church is not about people meeting together to hear a sermon. We meet in fellowship to worship God.

📱 Question 2: All believers in Jesus Christ belong to God's church and have a ministry and a purpose, even when they cannot go to a physical building. Jesus is not about buildings; instead, He is all about members being involved in love, good deeds, fellowship, encouragement, equipping the saints, and ministering.

STUDY 3: *Jesus is the Messiah.* (Chap. 2)

▪ The coming of Jesus was foretold when Adam and Eve committed the first sin.

▪ Question 1: Andrew knew who Jesus was because his heart was seeking God, and he had been prepared by the Holy Spirit to recognize the Messiah. The good news is that Jesus Christ is the Messiah, and he's come to free us from the bondage of sin.

▪ Question 4: Refer to John 15:26 and John 16:7-15 if needed.

STUDY 4: *Jesus is God's Son.* (Chap. 2)

▪ God makes Himself known to each of us in a unique manner.

▪ Question 3: Each Gospel writer had a specific audience in mind when they wrote their account of Jesus' life. Matthew was one of the disciples and a Jewish tax collector. He wrote for a Jewish audience. Mark, a fellow traveler with Paul, wrote for a Christian audience. Luke, also a traveler with Paul, was a Greek doctor and wrote for the Gentile, or non-Jewish, audience. John, the closest disciple to Jesus, wrote for both the Christian and the non-believer.

📖 Leader, read aloud Matt. 16:13-20, Mark 8:27-29, Luke 9:18-24. Make sure members understand that *all* Scripture is inerrant. Different accounts of the same events occurred because the Holy Spirit gave each writer a unique perspective to the events they knew of or had experienced.

STUDY 5: *Jesus is the source of our faith.* (Chap. 2)

📖 We can believe because God placed belief in our hearts. On our own strength we would not have the faith necessary to believe.

📖 *Easton's Illustrated Dictionary* explains *crucifixion* as: "A common mode of punishment among heathen nations in early times. It is not certain whether it was known among the ancient Jews; probably it was not. The modes of capital punishment according to the Mosaic law were, by the sword (Ex 21), strangling, fire (Lev 20), and stoning (Deut 21)."

The dictionary continues, "The condemned one carried his own cross to the place of execution, which was outside the city, in some conspicuous place set apart for the purpose... The accounts given of the crucifixion of our Lord are in entire agreement with the customs and practices of the Roman in such cases. He was crucified between two "malefactors" (Isa 53:12; Luke 23:32), and was watched by a party of four soldiers (John 19:23; Mat 27:36, 54), with their centurion. The "breaking of the legs" of the malefactors was intended to hasten death, and put them out of misery (John 19:31); but the unusual rapidity of our Lord's death (John 19:33) was due to his previous sufferings and his great mental anguish. The omission of the breaking of his legs was the fulfillment of a type (Ex 12:46). He literally died of a broken heart, a ruptured heart, and hence the flowing of blood and water from the wound made by the soldier's spear (John 19:34). Our Lord uttered seven memorable words from the cross, namely, (1) Luke 23:34; (2) Luke 23:43; (3) John 19:26; (4) Mat 27:46; Mark 15:34; (5) John 19:28; (6) John 19:30; (7) Luke 23:46."

For further insight, read, *He Chose the Nails*, by Max Lucado, (Word Publishing, Copyright © 2000).

CHAPTER THREE: *God provides Jesus as our Savior.*

Chapter 3 covers the who, what, why, when, and how of having a personal Savior.

STUDY 1: *What is a Savior?* (Chap. 3)

Jesus was the sacrifice necessary to save us from the eternal payment for our sins, that is, banishment from God's presence.

Question 1: Leader, have each member share an abbreviated version of his or her testimony. If someone does not remember a specific event of salvation, let their declaration at this meeting be the experience to treasure.

Question 3: The emphasis is on what *Christ* did for us so that we would be holy before a holy God. It is not about what we can do to make ourselves OK in God's eyes.

Question 6: The *old* refers to destructive behaviors and undesirable activities done before Christ was in your life. The *new* refers to attitudes and behaviors after being born again. Making mistakes and not being perfect are part of your Christian walk; these do not negate the newness of your life in Christ.

STUDY 2: *Where will I find my Savior?* (Chap. 3)

📖 Jesus waits until we invite Him into our hearts and lives. We need only believe and receive.

📖 Question 1: *Salvation* is described by *Easton's Illustrated Dictionary* as: "This word is used of the deliverance of the Israelites from the Egyptians (Ex 14:13), and of deliverance generally from evil or danger. In the New Testament it is specially used with reference to the great deliverance from the guilt and the pollution of sin wrought out by Jesus Christ, 'the great salvation' (Heb 2:3)." *Easton* also suggests finding out more about the terms *redemption* and *regeneration*.

📖 Question 3: Sheep behavior includes a mob mentality, a fear of the unknown, a timid and easily distressed spirit, a stubbornness to the point of stupidity, a proclivity towards perverse behavior, a helplessness in the face of disaster, an easily panicked temperament, an inability to cope with the unfamiliar, a willingness to butt heads, a restlessness when hungry or thirsty, and the tendency to blindly follow the leader. *A Shepherd Looks At Psalm 23,* by Phillip Keller, (Zondervan, Copyright ©1970).

📖 Question 6: Our mood does not affect our relationship with God—no matter how sinful we are nor how disgusted we feel with ourselves. It is our belief in Jesus Christ and *His* righteousness that brings us into the throne room of God, not our behaviors.

STUDY 3: *Who is my Savior?* (Chap. 3)

📖 The redeemer for our sins is Jesus Christ.

📖 Question 1: *Easton's Illustrated Dictionary* defines *peculiar*: "As used in the phrase 'peculiar people' in 1Pe 2:9, is derived from the Lat. peculium, and denotes, as rendered in the Revised Version ('a people for God's own possession'), a special possession or property. The church is the 'property' of God, his 'purchased possession'(Eph 1:14); R.V., 'God's own possession')."

📖 Question 2: *Easton's Illustrated Dictionary* defines *zeal* as: "An earnest temper; may be enlightened (Num 25:11-13; 2Co 7:11; 2Co 9:2), or ignorant and misdirected (Rom 10:2; Php 3:6). As a Christian grace, it must be grounded on right principles and directed to right ends (Gal 4:18). It is sometimes ascribed to God (2Ki 19:31; Isa 9:7; Isa 37:32; Ezek 5:13)."

📖 Question 3: Doing works that seem good to other people will not give one entrance into God's presence. Works that have the Holy Spirit's anointing are the only ones that will count. Works do not lead to faith, but rather through faith we do the good works God has planned for each of us.

📖 Question 6: The Jews were the chosen people of God. He specifically chose them to give them His laws. Paul's statement points out that, chosen or not, Jews still could not keep God's laws. Belief in Jesus Christ, however, gives eternal life to all who believe in His name, regardless of one's sins or whether they are Jew or Gentile.

STUDY 4: *How does my Savior save me?* (Chap. 3)

📱 Jesus died on the cross so that our sins could not keep us from Holy God.

📱 Question 2: Adjusting one's life-style to accommodate a chronic condition requires letting go of "perfectionism" thinking.

📱 Question 6: Leader, this line of inquiry may not be suitable or of interest to your participants.

Easton's Illustrated Dictionary informs us that "Trinity" is: "A word not found in Scripture, but used to express the doctrine of the unity of God as subsisting in three distinct Persons. This word is derived from the Gr. trias, first used by Theophilus (A.D. 168-183), or from the Lat. trinitas, first used by Tertullian (A.D. 220), to express this doctrine. The propositions involved in the doctrine are these: (1.) That God is one, and that there is but one God (Deut 6:4; 1Ki 8:60; Isa 44:6; Mark 12:29, 32; John 10:30). (2.) That the Father is a distinct divine Person (hypostasis, subsistentia, persona, suppositum intellectuale), distinct from the Son and the Holy Spirit. (3.) That Jesus Christ was truly God, and yet was a Person distinct from the Father and the Holy Spirit. (4.) That the Holy Spirit is also a distinct divine Person."

STUDY 5: *Why do I have a Savior?* (Chap. 3)

Jesus' sacrifice on the cross provides the bridge to our loving God who desires our eternal life to be spent with Him.

Question 3: Presenting the Gospel may seem complicated if a person is unprepared. Review the Gospel message:

1. God loves us. (John 3:16)
2. All of us have sinned. (Rom. 3:23)
3. Jesus died for our sins. (Rom. 5:8)
4. We must invite Jesus into our hearts. (Rev. 3:20)

CHAPTER FOUR: *God affirms that Jesus is the way to Him.*

Jesus' statement: *"No one comes to the Father except through me"* (John14:6) is controversial due to the exclusiveness it suggests. If one believes **all** the Bible is the word of God (2 Tim. 3:16), then Jesus' statement has to be true.

STUDY 1: *Jesus is the Way.* (Chap. 4)

Question 1: We Christians do not need all the answers to every question. Instead, we are empowered by the Holy Spirit who provides personal solutions to those of us who seek God with all our hearts. (Matt. 6:33)

Question 2: Many people agree with the viewpoint that Jesus Christ was a most revered prophet, an eminent teacher, and equal to Abraham, Moses, Muhammad, Gandhi, and Mother Teresa. All of these great people, however, died. Jesus Christ died but now He lives. Jesus Christ forgives sin. Jesus Christ is God. None of these other famous "good people" can make these claims.

Another misconception is that since Jesus Christ is the *Son* of God and spiritually equal to Satan. Some folks forget that Jesus **is** God, while Satan is only a fallen angel who is not all-powerful, is not all-knowing, and is not Creator.

Leader, build discussion of this question based on the fact that God's Word, the Holy Bible, is 100% true, that God cannot lie, and that Jesus Christ cannot lie. We dare not discard what we do not want to believe. Scripture hopping leads to people-made rules instead of God's grace in Jesus Christ.

STUDY 2: *Jesus is the Light.* (Chap. 4)

Question 2: *Easton's Illustrated Dictionary* defines what Biblical *grace* looks like with Scripture verses: "Favor, kindness, friendship are located in Gen. 6:8, Gen. 18:3, Gen. 19:19, 2 Tim. 1:9. God's forgiving mercy is found in Rom. 11:6 and Eph. 2:5. The Gospel is distinguished from the Law of Moses in John 1:17, Rom. 6:14 and 1 Peter 5:12. Gifts freely bestowed by God, such as miracles, prophecy, and tongues, are recorded in Rom.15:15, 1 Cor. 15:10, Eph. 3:8. Christian virtues are listed in 2 Cor. 8:7 and 2 Peter 3:18. And lastly, the glory hereafter to be revealed is told in 1 Peter 1:13."

Question 4: The Bible records a variety of methods Jesus used when healing, such as: driving out of evil spirits (Mark 5:6-8), touching a leper (Luke 5:12-13), healing when being touched (Mark 5:27-29), and restoring from a distance (John 4:49-52). This array of miraculous healings helps focus more on God's plan for our lives and less on finding that one-size-fits-all cure, the silver bullet, for our chronic condition.

STUDY 3: *Jesus is the Bread of Life.* (Chap. 4)

Question 4: Eternal life is not something we receive by our own efforts; it is something we receive by believing in Jesus Christ.

STUDY 4: *Jesus is the Vine.* (Chap. 4)

Question 2: God produces our fruit—it comes from the health of the vine. His perfect bunch of grapes—the results of His good works done through us—would metaphorically be mouth-watering, enormous, and delicious. Our fruit, however, is susceptible to other forces because we live in a sinful world. We have inner turmoil; we make worldly choices instead of Godly ones; we have an invisible enemy who tries to manipulate us through circumstances and relationships. Consider the paradox: our fruit comes from the trunk of the vine, Jesus; yet because we have free choice, we can influence the health of our fruit.

STUDY 5: *Jesus is the Resurrection.* (Chap. 4)

Question 1: The term *resurrection* as quoted from *Easton's Illustrated Dictionary*: "will be simultaneous both of the just and the unjust (Dan 12:2; John 5:28, 29; Rom 2:6-16; 2Th 1:6-10). The qualities of the resurrection body will be different from those of the body laid in the grave (1Co 15:53, 54; Php 3:21); but its identity will nevertheless be preserved. It will still be the same body (1Co 15:42-44) which rises again. As to the nature of the resurrection body, (1) it will be spiritual (1Co 15:44), i.e., a body adapted to the use of the soul in its glorified state, and to all the conditions of the heavenly state; (2) glorious, incorruptible, and powerful (1Co 15:54); (3) like unto the glorified body of Christ (Php 3:21); and (4) immortal (Rev 21:4)."

Question 3: Study Matt. 17:20 carefully. No matter what number you choose, God is still able to accomplish His purposes through your life.

GOD'S Rx SERIES

Book One: ***THE SILVER BULLET***
     Jesus Christ, Son of God
Chapter 1: God Declares Jesus Is His Son
Chapter 2: God Identifies Jesus With Many Names
Chapter 3: God Provides Jesus As Our Savior
Chapter 4: God Affirms That Jesus Is The Way To Him

Book Two: ***MAKE A LOUD NOISE***
     Complain or Praise
Chapter 1: Make A Loud Noise Or Sing A New Song
Chapter 2: Curse Your Enemies Or Bless Your God
Chapter 3: Victimized By Circumstances Or Rejuvenated By Praise
Chapter 4: Worldly Cares Or Heavenly Promises

Book Three: ***MOUNTAIN CLIMBING***
     Jesus, Our Mountain Climber Guide
Chapter 1: Jesus, Guide To Impossible Mountain Climbing
Chapter 2: Jesus, Escort Through Suffering
Chapter 3: Jesus, Encouragement Through Anxiety
Chapter 4: Jesus, Restoration To Climbers

Book Four: ***IN THE ARK WITH NOAH***
     Surviving Life's Storms
Chapter 1: Christ, The Creator
Chapter 2: Choosing
Chapter 3: Living Together
Chapter 4: God's Promises